Emotional Intelligence

Manage Your Emotions and Harness them for a Lifetime Full of Success

the solitary and utter responsibility of the recipient reader. Under no circumstances will any legal responsibility or blame be held against the publisher for any reparation, damages, or monetary loss due to the information herein, either directly or indirectly.

Respective authors own all copyrights not held by the publisher.

The information herein is offered for informational purposes solely, and is universal as so. The presentation of the information is without contract or any type of guarantee assurance.

The trademarks that are used are without any consent, and the publication of the trademark is without permission or backing by the trademark owner. All trademarks and brands within this book are for clarifying purposes only and are the owned by the owners themselves, not affiliated with this document.

Table of Contents

Introduction

I want to thank you and congratulate you for purchasing the book, *"Emotional Intelligence: Manage Your Emotions and Harness them for a Lifetime Full of Success"*.

This book contains proven steps and strategies on how to develop and increase skills and competencies that serve as the foundation of your Emotional Intelligence.

Understanding how your Emotional Intelligence develops by acquiring both personal and social skills in managing emotions will help you make sense of your own feelings – allowing you to harness them when making decisions or maintaining positive behaviors that will help you achieve your goals. Having high emotional intelligence helps you know yourself and the people around you better, creating lasting relationships and deeper bonds essential to reaching your full potential.

Thanks again for downloading this book, I hope you enjoy it!

Chapter 1: Defining Emotional Intelligence

The emergence of Emotional Intelligence as a form of *intelligence* has become widely known in recent times. From the conception of the term *Emotional Intelligence,* people have been encouraged to acknowledge their emotions and feelings more for the purpose of harnessing it for better understanding of their own experiences, and those of others as well. Behavioral studies have shown that in dealing with emotions as they come instead of suppressing them, people tend to be more rational in choosing how to express their feelings through their actions. To better understand Emotional Intelligence, one must know first how this type of intelligence is distinguishable from the well-known and established type of intelligence: The Cognitive Intelligence.

Cognitive Intelligence or IQ relates to the ability of people to think, understand, learn, and remember. It has been known to be a measure of the intelligence of a person and their thinking capacity. Many studies have proven that the IQ of a person can be a variable in attaining success in life. While it is a fact that people with above-average IQ thrive more in life when it comes to many different aspects of living compared to people having lower IQ, it is also true that people having the same IQ score does not necessarily mean that they will have the same level of success. This is where the difference in perceiving emotions with regards to reason comes in as a form of emotional intelligence.

Compared with the vast human knowledge on Cognitive Intelligence today, Emotional Intelligence or EQ/EI is a fairly new concept. With recent research, people are still coming to terms with it, especially since studies conducted on this type of intelligence have generated results essential to understanding human behavior and emotion.

Emotional Intelligence is comprised of the ability of the human brain to process emotions concerning your own self and others. Experiencing emotional response to circumstances means that the behavior of people are affected by their primary feelings and may be linked to making certain decisions that can elicit a strong impact on the course of life. These emotional influences may even be greater than that of the influence of the Cognitive Intelligence, which proves that Emotional Intelligence is as much of a factor in making life decisions. Each life event people experience has its own range of emotions, depending on the person experiencing them. One may experience loss, for example, as a life-altering event while some may view it as just another form of life process.

Regardless, the way people perceive and process emotions are not always the same and even uniquely their own. This factor only heightens the way with which Emotional Intelligence can gauge your understanding of your own self.

The part of the brain where emotions are experienced is called the Limbic System. For a human to rationalize a certain feeling, the emotion must first be processed in the front of the brain. Emotions perceived follow a pathway that starts from the spinal cord. Then, it is processed through the limbic system, which will lead to the rational thinking of the emotion experienced in the front of the brain. When there is effective communication between the rational and emotional parts of the brain, Emotional Intelligence is harnessed.

Harnessing your Emotional Intelligence is possible because emotions are fairly manageable and are easily influenced by events. Cognitive Intelligence, on the other hand, is instilled in the brain from birth and is immutable. It is not your intelligence per se (which, of course, can be improved by learning) but it is your *ability* to think. It is a definite part of your intelligence, under normal circumstances, and cannot be improved nor worsen. Your IQ score is permanent; its value is the same from when you were born to when you are in your sixties.

This means that while there are people who share the same IQ score, their rate of success differs because of many factors, one being the difference in their Emotional Intelligence. People of high intelligence may have a higher rate of securing themselves of brighter futures than those who have significantly lower IQs. But there are instances that the state of the emotional intelligence of people can affect their success rate no matter how high their cognitive intelligence might be. Take for instance people of above-average IQ with significantly low EI. They may have the necessary cognitive skills in running or managing a successful company but they also lack understanding of their own emotions and social relationships with their colleagues, resulting to poor communication and overall performance. Whereas people with average IQ but have high EI may be more sensitive to the needs of their colleagues and their own emotional stability in making rational decisions, for they are more capable of tapping into their experiences in eliciting the appropriate emotional response.

EI is a whole other fundamental part of your mind separate from intelligence. It is that particular medium of experiencing life by feeling or letting emotions govern behavioral decisions. In a way, it is choosing to allow emotions to partake in rational thinking to better understand a situation which requires people to delve deeper into different relationships or even with the self, instead of focusing on intellectual problem solving and facts. It is in its flexibility that managing emotions help in personal growth and success. By being aware of and practicing ways to manage your emotions, you will be able to harness your full potential and cope effectively to situations that warrant emotional involvement.

Dealing with your emotions and making them into productive thoughts and solutions instead of suppressing them is a way of polishing your emotional intelligence, which leads to making smart decisions and making the best choice out of all the choices you have. Understanding that this type of intelligence can be improved means that the way you make use of your EI determines your future in terms of the repercussions of your behavior towards an experience or event. It is important to manage emotions successfully so as to maintain a clear head under pressure and reign in possible outbursts due to over thinking and emotional overload.

Low EI may be attributed to poor relationships with family, friends or colleagues. Social involvement may be affected in having low EI, as well as awareness of your own emotional needs. Being intelligent does not necessarily mean that people already have the ability to manage their own emotions and feelings toward others. This means that a person of high intelligence may lack social graces and emotional stability. That said, being intelligent does not guarantee you to have the necessary skill to control your feelings and social behavior the same way as an emotionally intelligent person may not always have the cognitive ability to learn difficult tasks and solve problems.

The notable difference between IQ and EI may contribute to your success or failure. While IQ is fixed and having a low average score in that type of intelligence may hinder your success, by learning to manage emotions effectively to build better social relationships, self-awareness and confidence may yet be harnessed to make up for what a person may lack in achieving goals and aspirations.

As more and more people are becoming aware of Emotional Intelligence, it has become widely studied and researched. Many even have come to believe that it may be a more reliable measure of success than IQ. Due to its flexibility, ensuring growth in your EI can be achieved by managing your emotions and relationship with other people.

Chapter 2: Emotional Intelligence Competencies

Developing your Emotional Intelligence requires the necessary skills to manage your emotions and harness them for achieving success in life. In building a successful career, being *smart* when it comes to performing certain tasks is not enough. You need to be flexible and emotionally strong to cope with the people you are working with, to build productive relationships, and to be emotionally fit in facing many problems that will inevitably arise.

The skills involved in Emotional Intelligence have two categories. The first category is comprised of personal competencies or skills that deal with understanding your own emotions. The second category includes social competencies or skills that deal with your relationship with other people and how you manage your emotions toward them. This division of Emotional Intelligence into competencies was first coined by Daniel Goleman.

Personal Competencies

Self Awareness

This is your ability to recognize your own emotions and manage your tendencies and behaviors toward your own experiences. This means that you have the ability to perceive emotions the exact moment they happen. Being self-aware means that you are able to deal with your emotions and rationalize them into coherent thoughts. This includes being self-confident in deciding how to deal with difficult situations or with people whom you are not very comfortable with. Addressing negative thoughts can be difficult but allowing your brain to process them despite of the discomfort means a higher degree of self awareness.

Sometimes, it is not only the negative thoughts that people find difficult to deal with. Positive thoughts might be overlooked by some when negative thoughts are all they can think about. It is important to deal with both positive and negative thoughts as they come to mind for they each serve a purpose in managing emotions that improve overall self-awareness.

Being aware of your own self also means that you acknowledge your own flaws and shortcomings for the purpose of improvement. Managing emotions by focusing on your insecurities and imperfections does not mean that you are practicing self pity. It means that you have the skill to look past your flaws. Self-awareness propels you to take a chance on improving yourself.

Self Regulation

This is your ability to regulate your emotions based on acting on them efficiently as situations arise. Think of your emotions as the temperature of the water when you are taking a nice, long bath. You do not want the water to be hot enough to scald your skin nor do you want it to be cold enough to freeze you. You want the water to be nice and warm so you regulate the temperature to the level you desire. The same principle applies to your emotions. When a particular situation arises that warrants strong emotions, you have the ability to regulate them by allowing a sense of control to take over your brain.

Regulating your emotions will prevent the raging feelings from overwhelming you. This self control can tone down your own disruptive impulses to a minimum. Once you get past that overwhelming feeling clouding your mind, you can form coherent thoughts and solutions that were otherwise buried in your own tide of emotions. This provides you with the necessary control over your thoughts.

Self-regulation also includes trustworthiness. Above all, maintaining standards of honesty and integrity will help you reign in your emotions in the right way. It is also by taking full responsibility of your own actions and the consequences that come with them that you regulate yourself by being conscientious.

Your adaptability to changes and your flexibility to dire situations are components of self regulation. Avoid welcoming emotions of unproductive regret. Instead, focus your energy on adaptability to help you form legit decisions about things that you are unfamiliar with. Adaptability works well with being innovative and opening yourself to new ideas that will help you in achieving success.

Motivation

Motivating yourself is the start of achieving your goals. This means welcoming positive thoughts and having the drive to pursue your goals. This is a skill involved in improving your EI which will contribute greatly to your success in future endeavors. Committing yourself to a standard of excellence is a practice that will eventually become a habit; this is also called your achievement drive. Constantly strive to improve your work, even when you have only yourself to show for it.

Motivate yourself by making your goals in line with the goals of the company or the organization you belong in. This also involves having the initiative to grab opportunities as they come, for they are a means of preventing your days from becoming monotonous. Consequently, monotony limits the ways with which you can motivate yourself. One way of pursuing your goals despite of all the setbacks and obstacles that happen along the way is to be consistently optimistic.

Social Competencies

Empathy

The ability to gauge the emotions of other people and being attuned to what they may be feeling is important in being successful in your career, especially when you are constantly surrounded by people working toward the same goal as you are. It is an essential skill in building lasting social relationships. You will be able to elicit the right response to the behaviors of other people if you are sensitive to their emotions. Having the ability to understand others extends to being able to meet the needs of clients. This involves effectively anticipating their demands and delivering the right service.

Emotional Intelligence prides itself by being a type of intelligence that not only helps you cultivate your own capabilities, but also delights in having the competency to boost others as well. You are nurturing your own EI when you practice the ability to sense the needs of others and help them achieve progress by upholding their abilities. Developing others is one way of developing yourself as well.

People who are empathic also excel in being more open to new people and the diversity they may bring. Being exposed to different cultural views enriches your own cultural mind, thus allowing for more opportunities and diversity in your career. This includes political awareness and the competency to understand power relationships, making you more adept to the intricacies of different standpoints and emotional currents.

Social Skills

In a highly competitive workplace, having good interpersonal skills is a requirement. Business transactions flow smoothly when both parties exhibit good social graces. They are more likely to come up with an agreement that will benefit both in a successful partnership.

Successful dealings with people and colleagues are easily attainable when you know how to wield your influence in a persuasive and reasonable manner. People tend to listen more closely to others who have good command on the mutual language spoken. This involves the ability to weave what you want to say into conversations done casually. The message you want to relay is received accurately when it is delivered clearly and precisely. It is a sign of good communication when both parties understand each other thoroughly.

Working in groups or teams is a normal part of building relationships between people. There may be instances where your leadership skills will be needed. It is always good to be prepared to lead groups of people, especially when you have the ability to inspire and guide them during activities or projects. Emotionally-intelligent people usually have good leadership skills. They are attuned to the needs of others and have the capacity to influence them in making decisions that will contribute to the success of a project. Good leaders are also more adaptive to changes in plans or goals and may even initiate the said changes themselves. Good change catalysts must pursue changes that will bring success in the long run.

One important social skill is the ability to manage conflicts and resolve disagreements appropriately. Fair judgment must be practiced in dealing with conflicts and controlling damages. Nurturing bonds between people is one way of establishing lasting relationships. This is essential to gaining unity and respect when it comes to difference in ideals and beliefs. When deeper bonds form in social relationships, it is easier to collaborate and cooperate during projects and activities. Understanding the emotions of other people will lead to creating group synergy. This provides higher rate of success. In pursuing to collectively work towards a common goal, each member of a group contributes unique abilities and insights. The more useful ideas are presented to the group, the more likely it is to produce better outputs.

IQ alone cannot ensure success, no matter how high it is. In succeeding to achieve a certain goal, one must possess the necessary level of emotional intelligence as well. The intelligence innate to us will pave the way to better understanding of tasks in the most functional way. Better management of emotions, on the other hand, will help in ways that will guide you to efficiently perform tasks under pressure no matter how difficult they may seem.

Chapter 3 : Why is Emotional Intelligence Essential to Success?

Emotional Intelligence affects how people think. It is so influential that most of the decisions made by people, especially in workplaces, are based on emotions and rational thinking. Some may learn to shut their emotions off for days at a time to focus on a task at hand, but many choose to acknowledge them and even use it to their own advantage. This is a sign of having a high EI.

In a world where having a high IQ score is not enough anymore, many aim to uncover their emotional intelligence and harness it to their advantage. Attaining success involves having skills such as perseverance, self confidence, motivational drive, and good interpersonal skills. It is important to note that having a high EI means that you possess these skills and more. Businesses are run by people, and people ultimately are run by their thoughts and emotions. Understanding how EI contributes to success gives you the drive to tap into your own emotions in achieving your goals.

Between the two competencies and their many components discussed on the previous chapter, EI includes skills required to better understand emotions, both within you and with others. Many of these skills, if not all, contribute to success. The definition of success varies from different perspectives; some may define it as the achievement of financial goals while others simply view it as an intangible thing such as contentment and happiness. Whichever kind of success you are striving to achieve, know that a well-cultivated EI contributes to it since it focuses more on your emotional and rational thinking.

The following are some of the critical skills involved in Emotional Intelligence that are essential to success:

Accountability

Accountability is a form of self-awareness. It means the ability to hold yourself accountable for your own actions. It is when you take full responsibility and accept the consequences of the decisions you made. Accountability is making sure that you understand an idea well, which provides good communication and clarity. This means that you may be able to work on something the way your client wants exactly. It is an essential skill to have when it comes to being able to perform well in organizations that rely on good communication. Good communication involves understanding instructions appropriately and delivering the adequate information.

Assertiveness

This learnable skill is a mode of communication. It is the ability to state and demand your needs without having to resort to irrational and threatening behavior. It is a skill that can be nurtured. As a type of communication, it involves expressing yourself truthfully in a manner that does not involve forcing your beliefs down the throats of people. By being assertive, you are exhibiting respect for your own boundaries as well as others. By being open to cooperation with other people, you are making sure of getting want you want without harming others.

This skill is essential to success since it is required when dealing with people, especially when it comes to colleagues and clients. Assertive people tend to be freer in expressing their opinions and eventually get what they desire from others by being able to effectively compromise.

Change Tolerance

In the business world, change is constant. Maintaining a high tolerance to change is an essential skill to achieve success in the workplace that is constantly evolving. Accepting change and seeing it as an opportunity for growth makes it more tolerable. Consistency in business is important but being able to equip yourself with the right attitude towards change makes you all the more prepared for the progress it may bring. Do not hesitate to embrace necessary changes in all the aspects of your work or even the people around you. Opportunities may easily hold your way to success.

Decision-Making

Your emotions can affect your decision-making process. Anxiety, for example, may drive you to making rash decisions that might affect your desired progress in negative ways. Emotionally-intelligent people tend to make better decisions by focusing on the right emotions that arise in certain situations. By being able to identify emotions that will hinder proper decision-making, you will be able to disregard those emotions from leading you towards the wrong choice.

Studies have concluded that people are less likely to take risks due to anxiety that may not even be related to the risk itself. Success does not come without taking risks. It is important to be emotionally intelligent enough to know the difference between positive and negative emotions, and which kind is worth considering in making the right decisions.

Flexibility

In a way, flexibility is also being adaptable to change. In situations that involve doing things that are different from what they are used to, people with a sound emotional intelligence can cope by telling themselves they can do it. Refrain from thinking of ways in which a situation can go wrong. Instead, focus on everything that can go right. List down all the advantages of adapting to a new situation and use them as your achievement drive. Your emotional intelligence is affected by how adaptable and flexible you are to new situations.

Presentation Skills

Presenting your ideas effectively will ensure that you get your message or opinion across the way you want it received. Making the perfect pitch may be hindered by anxiety and nervousness, especially when facing a huge crowd. Having the ability to reign in unwelcome emotions and harness your self-confidence will help you present ideas efficiently. This will help you avoid any miscommunication by keeping a clear head and a well-organized thought process.

Having confidence in yourself in presenting ideas will help make people listen well to what you have to say. Developing that personal competency will harness not only your belief in your own abilities, but also the belief of others in your ideas.

Stress Tolerance

Self awareness is a skill that involves being able to handle stress well. In every aspect of the working world, daily challenges and obstacles contribute to overwhelming stress and discomfort. The lack of emotional intelligence may affect your stress tolerance and consequently, your role in being an effective player in the corporate world that strives for success. Performing well includes the ability to handle unstable situations that warrants a challenge in many aspects. Coping with stress by being optimistic and confident can be achieved by developing these emotional intelligence skills.

Teamwork

Developing your social competencies will help you create more lasting relationships with other people. Good relationships contribute positively to achieving work goals that require team work or working with other people. Having common goals help create more ways in which people can provide many insights and different ideas.

Having good social relationships is a sign of having a high EI. Developing these skills is essential to becoming successful in every field.

Time Management

With the strong ability to manage emotions as they happen, you can efficiently manage your time by lessening the amount of hours you spend over thinking. Distractions can occupy your mind when it is not equipped to handle unplanned situations that arise. The key is to hone your EI by managing emotions with rational thinking and disregarding useless thoughts that tend to take up so much time. Improving the way you manage yourself will help you in harboring more useful thoughts. Keeping other people from disrupting your schedule can be dealt with effectively through social awareness without compromising both your own work and your relationship with others.

Emotional Intelligence is the foundation of all these critical skills.

Harnessing your EI would mean having to develop these skills in contributing to your success.

Chapter 4: Develop Your Emotional Intelligence

People who can manage their emotions efficiently develop essential skills in both components of personal and social competencies. They are those who can handle the way their emotions affect their mood, behavior, and relationship towards other people in positive ways. These skills are most useful during times of trouble and finding solutions that can solve them. Knowing when to trust your intuition and believing in your abilities speak of having confidence in yourself. This will lead you to making the right decisions, especially under pressure.

Emotional Intelligence is inherent to people. This is a kind of intelligence that can be nurtured and developed. Tapping into your emotional and rational thinking will help you in more ways than just achieving your personal goals. It can lead you to the success of your career, allow you to form lasting relationships with other people, and give you better understanding of your own self.

- *Face your emotions head-on.* Filing away strong emotions every time a situation warrants it is like adding clutter to an already overflowing desk. Ignoring thoughts and emotions may mislead you into thinking that it will enable you to focus on a certain task at hand. In reality, you are only adding anxiety about having to deal with them later on. Pay attention to the emotions that arise about every situation and relate them to your experiences. This will help you behave appropriately based on the emotions you feel about something that happened, instead of caging in a lot of strong emotions. Suppressed feelings may lead you to express them all at once in a fashion that you will only regret in the future.

- *Acknowledge how your body manifests emotions.* Emotions,

while being processed in the brain, can manifest themselves in physical forms that you can feel in your body. Some may experience anxiety as a tingling sensation moving down the spine and having cold sweat. Anger may manifest itself as an uncontrollable bout of shaking and may induce tears in extreme cases. Fluttering in the stomach and the chest area may be due to joy and excitement. Sadness may be the cause of tiredness upon waking in the morning and throughout the whole day. Paying close attention to what your body tells you may help you gauge emotions that you did not know you were feeling otherwise.

- *Know where your emotions are coming from.* Knowing the cause of your emotions such as anxiety, stress, sudden anger, melancholy or excitement will help you behave in a rational manner in dealing with them. This will prevent you from blaming unrelated situations or people for the way you feel. You cannot solve a problem when you are addressing the wrong cause in the first place.

Understanding your emotions develops your EI. It is essential to reflect on your emotions first before reacting to a situation so that you may be able to react more appropriately when you experience the same feelings in the future.

- *Every emotion you have is worth feeling*. There is no such thing as a useless kind of emotion. Everything you feel, no matter how positive or negative it may be, has a purpose. Negative emotions may help you understand situations that may pose danger. This allows you to react with caution and discontinue harmful behaviors which may only worsen dire situations or hurt other people and yourself. Positive emotions, on the other hand, are even more important to fully feel and appreciate. By connecting emotions such as happiness, excitement, or contentment with certain experiences, you will be more prone to pursuing the same kinds of things in the future.

- *Learn from your emotions in the past.* Associate your emotions to past experiences and note their similarities and how you handled them before. It is unavoidable to feel strong emotions; they are usually the ones associated with extreme clarity in your memory. When a new situation arises that elicits strong emotions you have felt before, recall the previous times you have allowed yourself to feel them in the past, their impact in your life now and all the right and wrong ways you have handled them. This way, you will know how to make sense of familiar emotions and decide on ways in which you can use them to your advantage.

- *Let strong emotions pass before making decisions.* Callous decisions are often made when people are experiencing extreme emotions during situations well beyond their control. Exhibiting restraint is difficult when under the influence of emotions so strong they cloud your judgment. In cases like this, it is better to fully feel these emotions and let them wash over you first before doing anything you might regret. Decide how to behave and think of the possible outcomes of your behavior to reign in unreasonable actions from happening on your end.

- *Open your mind to new ideas and unfamiliar emotions.* Open-mindedness is a clear sign of having a high emotional intelligence. Narrow-minded people tend to close off their emotions and whole selves from experiencing new things, thus making them unable to adjust to any situation completely different from what they are used to. When you allow yourself to be open to possibilities, you are training your emotional intelligence to expand and improve when it comes to dealing with anything that might lead to success.

- *Be truthful with your own emotions*. People sometimes get used to lying about how they feel, especially when others are showing their concern. No matter how adamant you are in insisting that you are fine when you strongly feel otherwise, you will never convince yourself or other people who are observant enough. Practice being honest with how you physically show your emotions. This will help other people react appropriately around you without you having to pretend to feel fine when you are not. Share your happiness and excitement as well, the moment you feel them, for they also have a positive effect on people.

- *Practice being more empathic.* Improving your social

competencies helps develop your emotional intelligence. A person of high EI tends to be more observant about how others feel. Knowing how your actions may affect others will help you become more empathic. Develop empathy by putting yourself in their shoes; imagine yourself having to deal with their problems and what possible help they may need. Listen when people talk instead of just waiting for your turn to speak. Remember that there is much that can be learned from listening. Being sensitive to what others feel develops your ability to form more lasting social relationships.

Allow yourself to feel things as situations arise to become more equipped in reacting appropriately. It is in this way that Emotional Intelligence proves to be a form of *intelligence* since it makes you handle experiences wisely. EI can contribute greatly to success if you develop it and harness it to its full potential. People with high EI are easily the ones that can control their actions and are therefore, excellent players in the business world. Keeping these things in mind will help you develop what you already have and the potential hidden between your emotional and rational thinking.

Chapter 5: Increasing Your Emotional Intelligence

Unlike the fixed Cognitive Intelligence of people, Emotional Intelligence can be developed and raised. The ability of the brain to change is termed as *plasticity*. As discussed earlier, there is a pathway that connects your spinal cord to the front of the brain where the emotional and rational centers communicate in producing emotional intelligence. When you practice or develop new skills and competencies, you are strengthening this pathway. The billions of neurons lining this pathway branch off to connect to new cells formed when you learn a new emotional intelligence skill. This, however, does not happen overnight.

This branching out only happens when you develop a skill regularly. Each time you practice a new and improved behavior, you are making sure that this pathway is strengthened until that behavior becomes a habit, ultimately replacing the ones that you deem unproductive. Following this behavior, you are ensuring that your emotional intelligence grows as you acquire new skills.

Know and understand your own skills

Evaluate yourself and the skills you possess in both personal and social competencies. This is important in knowing which skills to develop and which skills you lack. Understanding your capabilities and accepting the possibility that you may not have it all is the first step in knowing how to increase your emotional intelligence. Seeing where you have room for improvement welcomes thoughts to take root in your consciousness and will eventually come out in the way you behave.

Self-assessment works effectively since you seek improvement yourself, instead of other people telling you what to do. The brain is a very powerful part of the human body. Learn to harness it to your advantage by grabbing the opportunity to increase your emotional intelligence by strengthening the pathway that connects emotional and rational thinking.

Personal competence may take a long time to develop. It is easier to attain when you accept yourself and your limitations. Improve your emotional intelligence from there by allowing your feelings to guide you in acquiring new behaviors. Use this skill to become good in your ability to use emotions to your advantage.

Eliminate your habit of suppressing emotions that bring you discomfort

The relief of burying uncomfortable emotions that plague your thoughts is short lived. No matter how many times you tell yourself to forget about them, they will eventually resurface. These may be behaviors that are unproductive and you would love to see gone from your habits. The good thing is you can train yourself to eliminate bad habits just as you can train yourself in acquiring new ones. And like acquiring new ones, eliminating bad behavior takes time.

Feelings never go away, even when you think you have successfully repressed them. When similar situations arise in the future, chances are, those emotions will resurface and you may not be able to handle them well. Deal with your emotions as they happen. The goal is to get through them no matter how hard it may seem. Once you get past them, you will find that you have made room for new and positive emotions.

Enable change by seizing the opportunity to do something productive about the emotions you feel. Emotions do not arise without reason. They mostly are the product of experiences and they all mean something other than unnecessary bother. Mostly when people suppress emotions, it is because they do not recognize them. The complexity of emotions will sometimes lead people into confusion on how to deal with them. Being able to recognize emotions is a sign of having high self-awareness. Training yourself to really understand what you are feeling makes it easier for you to manage it.

Motivate yourself by continuously training your brain

When you experience something that elicits strong emotions, chances are you will be motivated to adopt a new behavior. But the transiency of the emotion you experience limits your motivational drive to actually practice that behavior. You must train your brain to practice that behavior enough to make it last, otherwise you will no longer be as emotionally invested in acquiring that skill when your motivation fades. Find ways to remind yourself to feel that emotion again by writing it down. List all your feelings as you feel them and all the reasons you want to consider in choosing to pursue your goal. If the situation that drove you to develop a new skill came from a video, refresh your memory by watching it again.

Investing a huge amount of effort may be worth it when the behavior you want to acquire becomes a habit. This practice may take a while. It depends on the behavior you need to learn and the amount of time and effort you are willing to invest. Once this new behavior becomes a routine behavior, it is easier to maintain it because it will only take minimal effort to keep up something you are already used to doing. Deciding to do something is the starting point. Following through by motivating yourself will get you to the finish line.

Acquire new emotionally intelligent behaviors by understanding other people

Take note of the bad behaviors of other people and avoid practicing them yourself. People with low EI tend to be unaware of their bad behaviors and their tendency to be insensitive to the emotions of other people. When you find it hard to be comfortable with the way a person treats you, keep in mind to never practice that kind of behavior. Understanding how you want to be treated means you understand how to behave yourself around others.

Being able to tell what people mean by their body language and their non-verbal attempts at communication is a sign of having a good emotional intelligence. Trying to read what other people are feeling without them having to tell you is one way of enhancing your emotionally intelligent social skills.

Chapter 6: Taking Your Emotional Intelligence to Many Places

Our emotions are a part of us. They do not disappear or change suddenly when we are in different places. They influence the way you make decisions whether you are in the comfort of your home or in a fast-paced work environment. It is better to know how to handle them the moment they arise at the places you inevitably find yourself in.

Importance of Emotional Intelligence in the Workplace

The success of a business or an organization may depend on the way people work together in achieving a common goal. People with high emotional intelligence tend to work more efficiently together by being able to navigate the social complexities of the workplace. They are more likely to arrive with effective solutions to problems by being able to communicate well with each other. Co-existing with colleagues and other employees help with your performance as a working individual. Being sensitive to other people's emotions as well as your own will benefit the amount of work you will be able to accomplish in the workplace where team work is highly valued.

Emotions are present everywhere you go, regardless of what you do. In the event that strong feelings surface in the most hectic business hours, learn to manage them well by making them serve you instead of confusing you.

Being attuned to what other people are feeling is essential to having good communication. When an idea is presented well and received intact, the possibility of creating conflicts is minimized. Conflicts inevitably arise during bad handling of situations and the lack of proper communication.

Work through issues and problems one at a time and do not hesitate to ask for help. Your self-awareness is enhanced when you admit the need to improve yourself. Learn to accept help from willing colleagues to address an issue before it becomes too big to handle.

Engaging in teams creates an environment that gets the best performance from everyone, eliciting many different ideas and useful opinions. Members of emotionally intelligent teams relate to one another in making decisions and responding productively in uncomfortable situations. This allows each member to influence one another positively. Each member of the team can contribute constructively to the team effort by sharing their own different opinions and the same need for performing well. As a result, members of emotionally intelligent teams tend to experience a sense of satisfaction from working with others. The relationship formed between teams allows better management of their emotions as a whole.

Collective emotional management in teams is essential to their performance. As with individual management of emotions, a team experiences shared feelings that tend to influence decision making. Managing emotions as a whole the moment they surface in teams is crucial in managing relationship between each member. To arrive at a decision, a team must have a sense of unity and share the same feelings about a particular situation. This is where exhibiting social competencies in each member is important to have the emotional sensitivity towards other members of the group. Team emotional awareness is the result of how well each member of the group manages the emotions that influence their work.

When it is difficult to address your own emotions to come up with proper decisions, it is even more so when it comes to managing the collective emotions of a team. Pointing the team's varying emotional urges in the right direction is as essential as it is challenging. When every member has their own kind of emotion and in different intensities, it is sometimes next to impossible to name the exact emotion the whole team feels toward a certain project or goal. Allowing each member of the team to express what they feel is not always easy or productive. Knowing when to allow this is a good sign of team emotion management. The important step of feeling a collective emotion is to pair it with rational thinking. This ultimately means practicing team emotional intelligence. It is utilizing the collective emotions of a team to arrive at a performance essential for achieving overall team success.

Team emotional intelligence also includes both internal and external relationship management. Internal relationship management basically refers the ability of each member of the team to connect with other members based on the situation they are in. External relationship management, on the other hand, is the way the team deals with certain situations or projects as a whole.

Coming Home with Emotional Intelligence

The very foundation of a person is built first at home. It is where a person learns things before even learning in school. It is where people build relationships that are much deeper than the bond they form with others. It is not unknown that having trouble at home, most especially when it comes to being emotionally connected with your family, can impact your career and your life in general. Learning to form deeper bonds with your family is enhancing your emotional intelligence. Knowing that these people may be the only people that will stay throughout your whole existence is worth the lasting relationships you form with them.

Emotionally-intelligent couples tend to stay together longer than most.

Finding someone with whom you can be emotionally intelligent with for the duration of your life is not exactly easy. But once you do find someone, keeping that level of relationship as time wears on is where you can rely on your emotional intelligence to keep the fire burning. Having an emotionally-intelligent relationship means that both parties are willing to understand each other, to compromise when necessary, and to repair conflicts as they arise. Solving conflicts between two people is a sign of utilizing emotional intelligence skills.

Parents have a huge impact on the life of a child. The way parents manage emotion toward their children may influence their own emotional management as they grow old. Emotionally-intelligent parenting is essential to ensure a bright future. Regardless of how parents act, they ultimately are the role models of their own children. From them, a child learns the basic ways of the world. Children learn emotional intelligence skills from their parents. A parent's support can ensure that their child achieves their full potential and their high probability for success.

Whereas a child's IQ is gained from birth, emotional intelligence is not. These skills are made and developed. Parents have the first opportunity to develop their child's emotional intelligence. It may pave the way to their own management of emotional intelligence as they grow up to become active members of the field of shaping their own careers and success.

Your personal and professional life may not always be connected in terms of managing your emotions. You can be empathetic towards your family but quite distant when it comes to your colleagues. But emotional intelligence is the way you deal with your emotions as a whole, not just some distinct and separate parts of your life you wish to practice it on. It is the collective way you deal with yourself and others. A sign of having good emotional intelligence is your ability to utilize every skill you have and your flexibility in opening up to more positive behaviors in order to improve your life.

Conclusion

Thank you again for purchasing this book!

I hope this book was able to help you understand Emotional Intelligence and the ways with which it is essential for achieving your goals. In depth knowledge on EI can be made more useful when you apply it in your daily life from now on. New and positive behaviors in improving your EI may take a long time to achieve. Commit yourself to all the guidelines mentioned in this book to live your life successfully.

The next step is to practice what you learned from this book by keeping in mind all the necessary information and guidance it has given on how to manage your emotions and harnessing them for a lifetime full of success.

Finally, if you enjoyed this book, then I'd like to ask you for a favor, would you be kind enough to leave a review for this book on Amazon? It'd be greatly appreciated!

Thank you and good luck!